All we needed to say

Books by Marilyn Singer

Turtle in July
In My Tent
Sky Words
Family Reunion
In the Palace of the Ocean King
Charmed
All We Needed to Say

All we needed to say

poems about school from Tanya and Sophie

by **MARILYN SINGER**

with photographs by **LORNA CLARK**

ATHENEUM BOOKS FOR YOUNG READERS

Atheneum Books for Young Readers
An imprint of Simon & Schuster Children's Publishing Division
1230 Avenue of the Americas
New York, New York 10020

Book design by Ann Bobco
The text of this book is set in Deepdene and Univers Extended.

First Edition
Printed in the United States of America
10 9 8 7 6 5 4 3 2 1

Library of Congress Cataloging-in-Publication Data
Singer, Marilyn.
All we needed to say : poems about school from Tanya
and Sophie / by Marilyn Singer.—1st ed.
p. cm.
Summary: A collection of poems in which two girls, Tanya and Sophie,
express their differing opinions on gym class, library hour,
and other aspects of a day at school.
ISBN 0-689-80667-1
1. Schools—Juvenile poetry. 2. Children's poetry, American.
[1. Schools—Poetry. 2. American poetry.] I. Title.
PS3569.I546S36   1996
811'.54—dc20
95-32159

To my wonderful editor, Jonathan Lanman
—M. S.

For Stephanie and Deanie
—L. C.

Tanya

Before Mom can lift her lips
     from her morning cup of coffee
I'm out the door
     It's a race
         Mina and I run
to see who'll be first
     to greet Miss Tudeco at the crossing
         Mr. Lembersky at the door
First to breathe the squeaky aroma of chalk
         the drippy odor of poster paint
         the stink of stale spaghetti
         the fishy funk of feet
That old, old school smell
     I've learned to love
because I love to learn

Sophie

Late again
The principal calls me to her office
    that's pale pink
        but smells dark gray
  "Dawdling," she accuses
How can I tell her I was studying
    science:
        the shape of snowflakes
          landing on my glove
   math:
        the number of times
          Jane plus Julie plus Leigh
        will laugh at every boy they see
   reading:
        the new graffiti
          as wide as I am tall
        swirled across the faded school wall
  "It won't happen again," I say instead
Though I know for sure it will

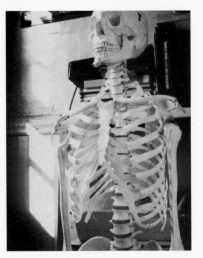

Sophie

Science class
     and Ms. Rothrock
asks, "How many things in this room
     come from the earth?"
To help me she holds up her chalk
     slaps the blackboard till it rattles
         (Slate, I think)
     kicks her desk and several chairs
         (Metal, wood, I know
           though I don't tell her)
"How many things in this room
     come from the earth?"
she repeats the question and waits,
     clicking her teeth
Repeats it again
     wiggling her ears
And still I don't answer
     or tell her what I'm thinking—
Not you, Ms. Rothrock
     Not you

Tanya

"There is no sound in space,"
        Ms. Rothrock says
And the idea is so amazing
        she says it once again,
"There is no sound in space."
        Comets crash into planets
        Giant suns explode
But on a ship drifting slowly
        through the stars
not a soul would hear them
        Or so Ms. Rothrock says
And I think I believe her
But someday, somehow I'd like to hear
        or not hear
            the silence for myself

Tanya

Nigeria   Morocco   Columbia   France
        The names of many countries
                striped and starred like flags
        wave from the walls in social studies class
For three weeks we have traveled the world
        meeting "Friends from Foreign Lands":
                Bulgarian boys who shake their heads no
                        when what they mean is yes
                Brazilian girls in the rain forest
                        munching crunchy bugs for lunch
                New Guineans painted and feathered
                        like fabulous birds
And I wonder could I really be friends
        with head-shakers
                insect-eaters
                        people dressed like creatures of the sky?
Could I ally with someone so different from myself?
        I think I'd like to try

Sophie

Teachers are like TV commercials
  saying the same thing over and over
    to sell you an idea
"Outside we're all different—
  Inside all the same"
is what Ms. Rothrock wants me to buy
  But I think she's got it inside out
Samoan boys in skirts
  Finns who feast on reindeer meat
Big deal!
  We all wear something
We all must eat
But people who hate baseball
  or people who like school—
Those are the differences that count
  Those are things that break her rule
and make it really hard
  to eat your lunch together
or play in the schoolyard

Sophie

In penmanship
  Tanya's capital Q's
    dip and swirl
  never a curl
    out of place
while mine droop and fret
   as though they got wet
     in the rain
I might like Tanya
   with her spotless dresses
   and her poodle hair
I might like Tanya
But I hate her capital Q's

Tanya

While Roddy reads aloud
    about a wondrous secret garden
in a voice as boring as a blank TV screen
I watch Sophie squirm in her seat
    and suddenly I think
she's like a garden, too
    a crazy quilt of flowers
      where tulips fight with roses
        asters argue with peonies
and a sign swings from "Keep Out"
    to "Come In" and back again
      in a flash
All the colors of the world
      clash
in Sophie's clothes
in Sophie's smile
    so full of yeses and noes
      stops and goes
she makes me dizzy
I don't know where she was
    or where she'll be
She's a place so busy
    I want to visit it
if only she'd let me

Sophie

My favorite word is
      somersault
My favorite class is
      gym
where Mrs. Marcy knows
      ropes are meant to be climbed
      balls to be thrown
      music makes everyone dance
And nobody says
      Sit down and be quiet
      You can't do that in here

Tanya

Who is first, last and in the middle?
The answer to this riddle
      is me
First in reading
        writing
        'rithmetic
Last to leave the library every day
And right smack in the middle in gym
I jump
        high on the trampoline
            But I don't soar
I sink
        one surprising basket
            But never four
There's nothing really
        bad
about being in the middle
It's just that it feels
        like you're fiddling around
            twiddling your thumbs
Because no matter how hard
        you try
You can't ever reach
        the sky

Sophie

Just in case we forget
It's Christmas
Easter
Halloween
Ms. Kyle the cook reminds us
with green cottage cheese
purple eggs
black and orange hot dogs
in black and orange buns
Today the meat loaf
bright red in slices shaped like hearts
says aren't you glad you brought those valentines—
and a brown bag lunch from home?

Tanya

Mom always taught me
    not to play with my food
But today in the cafeteria—
    where French fries are fangs
        buns become berets
        apples roll like bowling balls
          into empty Coke can pins—
I wanted to grab a handful
    of wriggling red Jell-O
        and hurl it like a shimmering cherry bomb
    clear across the room
    to startle the teacher
        custodian and cook
and most of all Sophie sitting there
      poking faces in her sandwich
      blowing soda at her friends
never knowing that I could maybe be
      as wacky wild
        as she

Sophie

In the library I slept
    dreaming of dragons
I read about in my bed the night before
    staying up late, so late to explore
        dark caves piled with sapphires and pearls
        and shining silver scales skimming
            shining golden worlds
    to smell the smoky choking breath
        as fire crackled in my hair
It felt, oh how it felt like I was there
In the library I slept
    dreaming of dragons
till Ms. Kagan woke me
    buzzing in my ear,
"Sophie, my dear, it's book time.
    Catch those z's at home."
I tried to grab a wing, a tail
    but they were gone, without a trace
I tell you school is not the place
    when you like to sleep in company
        but you like to read alone

Tanya

Hot cocoa warm and brown
      the library is my place
to cozy down
      and fly or sail or ride away
One day checking out moon rocks
      the next, searching for the Golden Fleece
One hour giving myself goosebumps
      another, bump-bump-bumping by a flock of geese
And oh the folks I meet
      sour, sweet
      smart and dumb
They welcome me
      I welcome them
Mi casa es su casa
      Your house is mine
And any place where I can read
      is home

Sophie

Mr. Feester said draw a picture
     of a place that you have been
But I've been nowhere
     except Uncle Irwin's house
          with the ping pong table
     and the dusty deer head
          that makes me want to cry
So instead I painted Paris
     with the Eiffel Tower
          sitting like a giant giraffe
     in the center of streets so bright and busy
          they glowed and wiggled off the page
In a happy rage
     I stayed past the bell to finish
When I looked up at last
     I was not alone
Tanya stood there, winking
     showing me her picture
          of a streamlined silver spaceship
     circling round the moon
          so bright and busy it glowed and wiggled
     off the page
"Someday," she declared
     "Someday," I agreed
Which was all we needed to say

Tanya

Aardvark, I call him
    whispering the word to Mina and to Sue
With his bulgy belly
    and bullhorn lips
there's nothing of the bird
    about Mr. Byrd
He never hops or flits
He blunders
    bumbling into our conversations
        our games of Double Dutch
    (which I cannot win)
       or hopscotch
    (which I can)
I want to like him
    the way I do

        Ms. Rothrock
        Mr. Feester
    and even the principal
        whom I hardly ever see
I want to like him
    because no one else does
But today when he stumbles into Sophie
    gunslinging insults with Mike
and arrests her
    like some tough dude sheriff on TV
I know I never will
Aardvark, I call him
    saying the word loud enough
for him to hear
He looks my way and smiles
    thinking I am not talking to him
Sophie looks and smiles
    knowing I am
Her face is like a valentine
    The best I ever got

Sophie

"Twice in one day," the principal sighs
And this time I try to explain
      the difference between a curse that kisses
           and a curse that smacks
Total geek
      Fatso, freak
hurt worse than sticks and stones
But scumsucker
      Pigmucker
Kitty litter baby sitter
      those words don't prickle
They tickle
      making me and Mike giggle
when we shout them at each other
      clear across the schoolyard
that's so noisy I can't think
      how Mr. Byrd ever heard
         a word we said
"I see," the principal says
And maybe she does
      'cause she's smiling when she warns us
never to swear
      not even with flair

Sophie

Ruh. . .ing, the three o'clock bell stutters
        ("Still broken," Ms. Rothrock mutters,
                the way she does every day)
And I stand slug slow
        for once in no hurry to go
though I'm not sure why
        Maybe I'm still seeing
                the glittery glow of Paris
                the principal's sideways smile
        or poodle-perfect Tanya saying "Aardvark"
                to that turkey Mr. Byrd
Three small surprises in one day
        And four is on the way
Without a word I glide
        to Tanya's side
and we stroll away
        with Mina in tow
Maybe I'll show her
        how I study snowflakes
or point out the graffiti on the wall
        Maybe I won't talk at all
And in the morning we'll set off together for school
        That is, if I'm not late
Or perhaps if Tanya can wait

Acknowledgments

The photographer acknowledges the following faculty and students who were helpful in preparing the photographs for this book: *PS3, Principal*: Lesley Gordon, *Teachers*: Alan Tung, Andrea Schwartz, Diane Mullins, Carole Randall, Dan Zulawski, Marcy Mazzetti, *Students*: Miranda Rhyne, Nora Domenas, Sylvia Khrumana, Tina Miller, Gem Carter, Chakisha Carriman; *East Side Middle School, Director*: Lawrence Hirsch, *Students*: Una Osato, Sonja Mereu; *St. Angela Merici School, Principal*: Patrick Kelly, *Students*: Julissa Jimenez, Fallon Ellis; and Philip Dolin.